DOMINOES

STARTER LEVEL   **250 HEADWORDS**

Great Clarendon Street, Oxford, OX2 6DP, United Kingdom

Oxford University Press is a department of the University of Oxford.
It furthers the University's objective of excellence in research, scholarship,
and education by publishing worldwide. Oxford is a registered trade
mark of Oxford University Press in the UK and in certain other countries

2018

10 9 8 7 6

ISBN: 978 0 19 424913 3   Book
ISBN: 978 0 19 463925 5   Book and Audio Pack

Printed in China

This book is printed on paper from certified and well-managed sources

ACKNOWLEDGEMENTS

The publisher would like to thank the following for permission to reproduce photographs: Alamy
Images pp.24 (Winding mountain path/fStop), 31 (Old book/Eclipse), 44 (Mount Fuji/Gavin
Hellier); Corbis ppiv (Rocky Mountain National Park/Richard T. Nowitz), 39 (Alpine aster/
Stuart Westmorland), 43 (Gornergrat Bahn cog train/Patrick Frilet/Hemis); Getty Images
pp iv (Farmhouses in Italy/Andreas Strauss), iv (Boathouse at Lake Zeller, Austria/Andreas
Strauss), iv (St. Magdelena village and church/Gavin Hellier), 7 (Regional Natural Park of
Monti Simbruini/DEA/R. CARNOVALINI), 43 (The Matterhorn/Daisy Gilardini)

Cover: Getty Images (Mountain hut/Tyler Stableford/Riser)

Illustrations by: Monica Armino/Advocate Art

DOMINOES

Series Editors: Bill Bowler and Sue Parminter

Heidi

Johanna Spyri

Text adaptation by Paul Davenport
Illustrated by Monica Armino

Johanna Spyri (1827–1901) was born in a village in the Swiss Alps, and grew up in the Swiss countryside. She moved to Zurich to study, and married her husband – a lawyer – there in 1852. Unhappy in the city, Johanna began writing stories about places she knew as a child. Her best-known story – *Heidi* – first appeared in German in two books (1880 and 1881). It was very successful then, and is still popular around the world today – as a book, on TV and in the cinema. Johanna died in Zurich, aged 74.

OXFORD
UNIVERSITY PRESS

ACTIVITIES

BEFORE READING

1 Match the words with the pictures. Which is your favourite season? Why?

autumn   spring   summer   winter

a ....   b ....

c ....   d ....

2 The story happens in the 1800s in Dorfli, a village in Switzerland, and Frankfurt, a big town in Germany. Read sentences a–f and write D (Dorfli) or F (Frankfurt).

a ☐ It snows a lot in winter.   d ☐ Young children don't go to school.

b ☐ There are many big houses.   e ☐ There are many people with a lot of money.

c ☐ Many people can't read or write.   f ☐ Life is very quiet.

Chapter 1 ❧ Heidi arrives

One June morning, a young woman and a little girl are walking up a **mountain** in Switzerland. When they **reach** the village of Dorfli, an older woman calls to them.

'Dete! Where are you going? Is that the daughter of your **late** sister?'

'Yes, Barbel. I'm taking her to her grandfather.'

'Please don't! He's very **strange** these days. He never visits the village, and he speaks to nobody.'

'But I've got new work in Frankfurt. I can't **take care of** Heidi now.'

Just then, Peter the young **goatherd** arrives. He takes Dete and Heidi up to the old man's **hut**.

'Here's your granddaughter – Heidi,' says Dete when they arrive. 'She must stay with you. I can't take care of her any more.'

'What?' the old man cries. 'Get out of here, Dete! And don't come back!'

'Goodbye, Heidi,' Dete says. She goes quickly down the mountain. Peter goes back to his goats.

Heidi looks about her. 'Oh, Grandfather, it's beautiful up here!' she says. The old man says nothing, but he takes her into the hut.

mountain a big hill

reach to arrive in a place after travelling for some time

late dead

strange not usual

take care of to do things for somebody when they need it

goatherd a boy who looks after goats

hut a little house

Heidi finds a wonderful room there: the **hayloft**! All that afternoon, Grandfather makes a little chair for Heidi. That evening she sits in it at dinner. She loves it!

That night, there is lots of **wind**. Grandfather goes up to the hayloft. Heidi is sleeping there. He smiles when he sees this and goes down to bed happily.

Early the next morning, Peter comes to the hut for Grandfather's **goats**.

'Can Heidi come up the mountain with me?' he asks the old man.

'Do you want to?' Grandfather asks Heidi.

'Yes!' she answers.

'Take good care of her!' Grandfather tells Peter.

Up on the mountain, the goats eat hungrily. Peter **lies down** and sleeps. Heidi doesn't sleep. She looks at all the beautiful blue and yellow flowers.

hayloft a room at the top of a country home where you put hay (dry grass)

wind air that moves

goat an animal that lives on the mountains

lie down (*past lay*) to have all your body on the ground

Later, Peter sits up. '**Lunch** time!' he says. Heidi gives some of her lunch to him because he hasn't got much.

Suddenly Peter gets up. One of the goats is near a **cliff**! Peter begins to run to it, but he **falls** down. Quickly, Heidi **picks** some flowers and calls the goat. It comes to her, and away from the cliff. Peter begins hitting it angrily.

'Stop!' Heidi cries.

'Can I have some of your lunch tomorrow?'

'Yes, and every day – but **promise** me one thing: never hit a goat again.'

'All right,' Peter laughs.

◖◗

lunch when you eat in the middle of the day

cliff a wall of rock on a mountain that you can fall down easily

fall to go down suddenly

pick to take things like flowers or apples from plants or trees

promise to say now that you can do something later; when you say that you can do something later

3

Back in Grandfather's hut, Heidi talks about her wonderful day. Not long after that, she is sleeping happily up in the hayloft.

Every day, Heidi goes up the mountain with Peter. But soon the days are colder. In **winter** Peter must leave the mountains and go to school in Dorfli. He doesn't like that!

One day, Peter comes up to the hut. 'Can Heidi visit us? My grandmother wants to meet her,' he says.

'Of course she can,' Grandfather says.

))◦((

Two days after that, Grandfather takes Heidi to Grandmother's little house.

'Hello! It's me, Heidi!' she calls at the door.

'Oh, Heidi! Come in. Peter talks about you a lot,' the old woman says. 'Brigitte!' she asks her daughter. 'Can you look at Heidi and tell me all about her?'

'She's beautiful, Mother!'

'Grandmother, can't *you* see me?' Heidi asks.

'No, Heidi. My eyes don't work. I can't see a thing.'

Heidi begins to cry at that, but the old woman says, 'Don't cry. Tell me, do you like living with Grandfather?'

Suddenly, there is a **loud** noise in the house. 'Listen to that! This old house is falling down, I tell you!' Grandmother says.

'Mother can't sleep at night because the house moves in the wind,' says Brigitte.

))◦((

Back home, Heidi asks Grandfather, 'Can you **fix** Grandmother's house? Please!'

In the end, he says yes. After that, when Heidi visits Grandmother, Grandfather goes too and works on the

winter the three coldest months of the year

loud making a lot of noise, not quiet

fix to make OK again

house. Soon it is OK, and Grandmother can sleep well in her bed again.

pastor a person who works for the church

These are happy times for Heidi. But, after two years, the village **pastor** visits Grandfather's hut one day. He looks at Heidi and Grandfather, and he doesn't smile. 'Why am I here?' he asks them. 'Do you know?'

READING CHECK

Match the sentences with the people in Chapter 1.

| Heidi | Peter | Grandfather | Grandmother | ~~Dete~~ | Brigitte |

a ..... Dete ..... takes Heidi to live with her grandfather.

b .... gives some of her lunch to Peter in the mountains.

c .... doesn't like going to school.

d .... can't see a thing.

e Peter's mother's name is ....

f Heidi's .... works on Peter's grandmother's house.

WORD WORK

1 Find words from Chapter 1 to match the pictures.

a cliff   **b** g _ _ _   **c** h _ _   **d** l _ _ _ _

e g _ _ _ _ _ _ _   **f** m _ _ _ _ _ _ _   **g** h _ _ _ _ _ _   **h** p _ _ _ _ _

2 Use the words in the flowers to complete the sentences.

a I .take. care. of. my brother when my parents are working.

b Please don't . . . . the flowers. Leave them there.

c Heidi asks her grandfather, 'Can you . . . . Grandmother's house?'

d It's late. You must . . . . and go to sleep.

e Can I have some of your lunch every day? Do you . . . . ?

f Suddenly they hear a . . . . noise in the house.

GUESS WHAT

What happens in the next chapter? Tick one box.

a ☐ Heidi and Grandfather move to the village of Dorfli in winter.

b ☐ Heidi goes to Frankfurt with Dete.

c ☐ The pastor takes Heidi away from Grandfather's hut.

Chapter 2 ❧ Heidi's new family

'Heidi's nearly eight now,' the pastor says. 'When winter comes, she must go to **school**.'

'Through all the **snow**? I can't **send** her down the mountain then,' Grandfather says.

'No,' the pastor smiles, 'But you can come down and live in your old house in Dorfli this winter. Heidi can easily go to school from there.'

'Never!' Grandfather says. 'The villagers don't like me!'

'That's not true,' answers the pastor. 'Please come back to the village this winter.'

'I can't,' Grandfather says. The pastor leaves soon after. He is not happy.

‹◖ ◗›

The next day, **Aunt** Dete arrives at the hut.

'Why are *you* here?' cries Grandfather.

'For Heidi,' she says. 'Listen! I'm working for a nice family in Frankfurt. One of their friends – **Herr** Sesemann – has

school students learn here

snow something soft, cold and white

send to make someone go somewhere

aunt your mother's (or father's) sister

Herr /heə(r)/ Mr in German

lots of money, but his daughter, Clara, is very ill. She's in a **wheelchair**. Herr Sesemann's often away for work, and Clara **misses** her late mother. She needs a young friend. Heidi can come and live in their wonderful house, play with Clara, wear beautiful things, and learn–'

'Stop!' Grandfather says angrily.

But Dete doesn't stop. 'Heidi's nearly eight and she can't read or write. She can't stay here!'

Grandfather looks at Dete darkly. 'Then take the child and go,' he cries, 'but I never want to see her here again!' And he quickly leaves the hut.

'I'm not going with you, Aunt Dete!' Heidi cries.

'Oh yes, you are!' Dete answers.

She takes Heidi by the hand and she **pulls** her down the mountain.

Two days later, they arrive at the Sesemanns' house in Frankfurt. Clara likes Heidi at once, but **Fräulein** Rottenmeier, the **housekeeper**, wants to send her away.

wheelchair a chair with wheels for somebody who can't walk

miss to want something that you don't have now

pull to move something nearer you

Fräulein /ˈfrɔɪlaɪn/ Miss, an unmarried woman, in German

housekeeper a woman who looks after someone's house

'Clara's twelve,' she says. 'So how can a little girl of eight be her friend? Take her away!'

But Aunt Dete says goodbye quickly, and Heidi stays.

Heidi likes Clara a lot, but she misses her home in the mountains. From her window she can only see houses.

One day, she runs out into the streets of Frankfurt and looks for a **tower**. Perhaps from there she can see better?

In the end she finds a tower, and a nice man there takes her up it. But what can she see when she looks across the town? More houses!

tower a tall building or part of a building

kitten a very young cat

'Oh!' she cries. 'Where are the mountains?'

The man says, 'There are no mountains here, but I've got some **kittens** in my room. Would you like some?'

'Yes, please!' Heidi cries.

He gives two kittens to Heidi. She puts them in her **pockets** at once and then walks quickly back to the Sesemanns' house.

When she arrives, Fräulein Rottenmeier is very angry.

'You must never leave the house again **alone**, you bad girl!' she says,

Suddenly, she hears a strange noise from Heidi: 'Meow!'

'What's that?' cries Fräulein Rottenmeier.

'My kittens,' Heidi smiles. She takes them out of her pockets.

'Ugh! Take them away!' Fräulein Rottenmeier cries. She doesn't like cats.

Clara likes the kittens, so they stay. But, after that, the housekeeper is more and more **unfriendly** to Heidi, and Heidi feels more and more **homesick**.

'I must leave soon!' she thinks.

After some weeks, she is ready.

Early one morning she is walking out of the front door when someone behind her says, 'And where are *you* going?' She looks back slowly and – oh, no! – Fräulein Rottenmeier is looking at her with angry eyes!

pocket the place in your coat or dress where you can put things

alone with nobody

unfriendly not nice

homesick when you don't feel happy because you are away from home

11

READING CHECK

Are these sentences true or false? Tick the boxes.

		True	False
a	The pastor wants Heidi and Grandfather to live in Dorfli.	☑	☐
b	Dete goes to Grandfather's hut and takes Heidi away.	☐	☐
c	Grandfather is happy when Heidi goes to Frankfurt.	☐	☐
d	Heidi lives in her aunt's house in Frankfurt.	☐	☐
e	Heidi goes to Frankfurt because Clara Sesemann needs a friend.	☐	☐
f	One day, Heidi goes out and comes back with two little dogs.	☐	☐
g	Heidi likes Clara, but she wants to go home to the mountains.	☐	☐

WORD WORK

1 Complete the puzzle with the words from Chapter 2.

ACROSS →

DOWN ↓

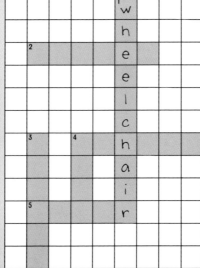

2 Find words from Chapter 2 in the snow.

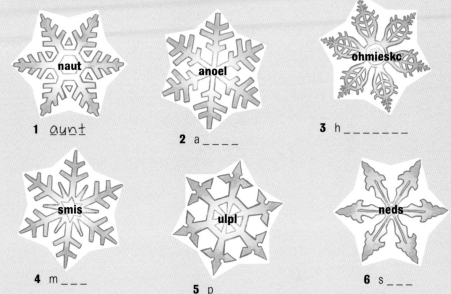

naut

anoel

ohmieskc

1 aunt

2 a _ _ _ _

3 h _ _ _ _ _ _ _

smis

ulpl

neds

4 m _ _ _

5 p _ _ _

6 s _ _ _

3 Use the words from Activity 2 to complete these sentences about the story.

a ..... Aunt ..... Dete is Heidi's mother's sister.

b 'Do you .... the mountains?' Clara asks Heidi.

c Fräulein Rottenmeier is angry when Heidi goes out ....

d Grandfather doesn't want to .... Heidi away.

e Heidi wants to see the mountains and she feels .... in Frankfurt.

f Do you want to open that door? You need to .... it.

GUESS WHAT

What happens in the next chapter? Tick three sentences.

a ☐ Heidi goes home to Switzerland.

b ☐ Fräulein Rottenmeier speaks angrily to Heidi.

c ☐ Herr Sesemann sends Heidi away from his house.

d ☐ Heidi learns to read with the help of Clara's grandmother.

e ☐ Heidi walks in her sleep.

f ☐ Clara feels happy to be alone again.

Chapter 3 Homesick

'Answer me, girl! Where are you going?' the housekeeper asks Heidi angrily.

'Home,' Heidi answers.

'But this is your home now! Do you want to leave Clara here alone?'

'No,' Heidi says. 'But I must go to Grandfather. I miss him, Peter, Grandmother, the goats – and the mountains. I can't live without them.'

The housekeeper's face is very red now. 'You bad child!' she cries. 'Go to your room this minute, and *never* leave this house again!'

A day or two later, Clara calls Heidi to her room. 'My father's back home,' she says happily, 'and he wants to speak to the two of us.'

Just then, Herr Sesemann comes in. He takes Clara in his arms. After that he has a nice talk with her and Heidi. Then he smiles and leaves them.

He goes to Fräulein Rottenmeier and tells her, 'You're wrong about Heidi. She's not a bad child. Clara likes her very much, and Heidi's good for my daughter,' he says.

'But –' Fräulein Rottenmeier begins.

'So don't tell me any more stories about the little Swiss girl. Do you understand?' Herr Sesemann says.

'Yes, Herr Sesemann,' Fräulein Rottenmeier answers.

'Now, I'm leaving again for work in two days, but my mother's coming soon. I don't want any **problems** when she's here,' he says.

'No, Herr Sesemann,' the housekeeper says.

《◎ ◎》

Grandmamma Sesemann loves Heidi when they meet, and she is very good to the little girl. She gives some picture books to her and with her help, Heidi soon learns to read. Heidi loves reading. With a book in her hands, she forgets that she is homesick.

problem
something that makes you feel bad

grandmamma
an old word for 'grandmother' from the 1800s, often used by children from rich families

15

Clara and Heidi are happy when Grandmamma Sesemann is staying with them. But after she leaves, Heidi feels more homesick than before.

Some days later, strange things begin to happen in the Sesemanns' house. Every morning, the front door is open! Fräulein Rottenmeier tells two of the **servants**, 'Perhaps it's a **ghost**. You must watch the **hall** tonight and see.'

When they later see something white in the dark hall, they run and tell the housekeeper.

She writes to Herr Sesemann that night:

Strange things are happening here!

Please come home!

servant a person who works for someone rich

ghost a dead person that a living person hears or sees

hall a big room near the front door of a house from which you can go to all the other rooms

doctor (before family name **Dr**) this person helps people when they are ill

nightdress a long dress that girls and women wear to go to bed

Herr Sesemann arrives the next afternoon and speaks to the servants. They tell him about the white thing in the dark. After that, he has a long talk about ghosts with a **doctor** friend of his, Dr Classen. Late that night, they suddenly hear a noise in the hall. What is it? They go and look. There, by the open door, stands Heidi in her white **nightdress**. She is walking in her sleep!

'Heidi!' Herr Sesemann cries. 'What are you doing here, my child?'

She opens her eyes. 'Where am I?' she says.

'Leave this to me,' Dr Classen tells Herr Sesemann. He takes Heidi to her room and talks to her quietly there.

'You aren't happy. What's the problem?' he asks.

At first she tells him nothing, but in the end she says, 'Every night I **dream** about my mountain home. I hear the wind, and I go to the door of the hut and look out. But in the morning, I'm back in Frankfurt.' She begins to cry.

'Don't cry, little Heidi,' says the doctor. 'Every problem has an answer.'

He goes back to Herr Sesemann. 'Heidi's very ill,' he says. 'She must leave for Switzerland at once!'

dream to see pictures in your head when you are sleeping

READING CHECK

Choose the correct words to complete the sentences.

a Fräulein Rottenmeier is angry and she sends Heidi to *Switzerland / her room*.

b Clara's father talks to Fräulein Rottenmeier about *Heidi / the kittens*.

c With help from Clara's *grandfather / grandmother*, Heidi learns to read.

d Heidi feels *homesick / ill* after Clara's grandmother leaves.

e Some days later, the *front door / window* is open in the morning.

f The servants see something white in the *garden / hall* at night.

g Fräulein Rottenmeier tells Herr Sesemann, 'Please *come home / go away*.'

h They see *Clara / Heidi* in the hall in her white nightdress.

i Heidi *walks / talks* in her sleep because she isn't happy.

j 'Heidi must go to *Frankfurt / Switzerland*,' Dr Classen says.

WORD WORK

Correct the mistakes in these sentences using words from Chapter 3. Use the pictures to help you.

doctor

a Heidi talks to the ~~daughter~~.

b 'Give that to the student.' ....

c There's a goat in the house. . . . . **d** Let's go into the wall. . . . .

e She's in a white evening dress. . . . . **f** She drives about mountains. . . . .

GUESS WHAT

What happens in the next chapter? Tick two boxes.

a ☐ Clara goes to the mountains with Heidi. **b** ☐ Grandfather is happy to see Heidi.

c ☐ Heidi reads to her grandfather. **d** ☐ Peter goes and lives in the pastor's house in the village.

19

Chapter 4 ❦ Home again

What can Herr Sesemann do? Heidi can't stay ill, but Clara can't lose her friend. In the end, he finds the answer to this problem. He speaks to the two girls.

'You're very homesick,' he tells Heidi, 'And you need to **return** home to the mountains. Dr Classen says this, and he's right, I think.'

'But Father –' Clara begins.

'Please, Clara,' says Herr Sesemann, 'Let's think of Heidi now. What's best for her? But I promise you, daughter, you can visit her in Switzerland very soon.'

Then he says to Heidi, 'So are your bags ready? Because your **journey** home begins early tomorrow morning!'

return to go back; when you go back

journey when you go far

❦

Two days later, Heidi arrives at the village of Dorfli. Before she goes to her grandfather's hut, she visits Peter's house. She gives nice **presents** from Clara to Peter's mother and grandmother.

'Thank you!' they say. 'Now please don't go!'

'I must. But I can come back tomorrow,' Heidi promises. Then she **hurries** up the mountain.

When she reaches her grandfather's hut, she calls, 'Grandfather! It's me, Heidi! I'm back!' Grandfather comes out of the hut and looks at her. He is very **surprised**. Suddenly, he takes her in his arms and he laughs.

'Heidi. Is it truly you?' he cries.

The next day, Heidi goes and sees Grandmother again. 'Well, do you like living in Frankfurt?' the old woman asks. Heidi tells Grandmother all about it. Suddenly, Heidi remembers something, and she laughs.

'Oh, and I can read now!' she says. 'Can I read to you?'

'Yes, please!' answers Grandmother.

For the next hour, Heidi reads to her. 'You can read beautifully!' the old woman says when she finishes.

present
something that you give to someone

hurry to do something quickly

surprised
feeling that something very new is suddenly happening

Back at Grandfather's hut, Grandfather gives a big, old book to Heidi and he says, 'Read to me from this.'

She opens the book and reads a wonderful story to him.

Once a young man leaves home and goes to a far town. At first he has lots of money and many friends there. Then he loses all his money and his friends, and he is alone and **sad**. In the end he returns home with nothing. But his father isn't angry. 'Here's something nice to wear, and something good to eat,' the old man says — because he feels happy to see his son again.

When Heidi stops reading, Grandfather is very quiet.

The next morning – Sunday – he takes Heidi to **church**. The people there are very surprised when they see him arrive with his granddaughter.

After they leave the church, Grandfather goes to the pastor and says, 'I'm coming to live in the village this winter. Heidi can go to school more easily from here.'

'Good!' smiles the pastor.

sad not happy

church Christian people go here to pray

Back in Frankfurt, Clara asks Herr Sesemann every day, 'Father, when can we visit Heidi?'

He always answers, 'Soon, daughter, very soon.'

But when he thinks about the long journey, he feels afraid. 'Is it a good **idea** for Clara to go?' he thinks.

In the end, he speaks to Dr Classen about it.

'Doctor,' he asks, 'Can Clara visit her friend Heidi in Switzerland this **autumn**?'

The doctor answers sadly, 'No, she can't. The journey is long, and your daughter isn't very **strong**. You must be very careful with her. I know this story well. Remember last **spring**. I'm alone now because *my* young daughter is dead. But I can never forget her.'

idea something that you think

autumn the three months of the year before winter

strong with a body that works well

spring the three months of the year after winter

READING CHECK

Match the two parts of the sentences.

a Herr Sesemann promises Clara, ...
b Heidi arrives in the mountains ...
c Heidi stops at Peter's house ...
d When Grandfather sees Heidi ...
e On Sunday, Grandfather and Heidi ...
f The village people are surprised ...
g In Frankfurt, Clara is sad because ...
h Dr Classen tells Clara's father, ...

1 and leave some presents there.
2 go to church in Dorfli.
3 'Clara can't go to Switzerland.'
4 'You can visit Heidi in Switzerland.'
5 he takes her in his arms.
6 she misses Heidi.
7 two days later.
8 when they see Grandfather in church.

WORD WORK

1 Find ten more words from Chapter 4.

2 Use the words from Activity 1 to complete the sentences.

a Clara sends ..p̲r̲e̲s̲e̲n̲t̲s̲.. for Heidi's friends.

b The .... from Frankfurt to Switzerland is very long.

c The pastor works in the village ....

d 'We're late. Please ....!'

e Heidi must .... to Switzerland, but Clara isn't happy about it.

f In .... there are many beautiful flowers on the mountains.

g 'Don't be ...., Clara,' Heidi says, 'You can visit me.'

h Grandfather is .... when Heidi comes home.

i The mountain trees are many different colours in ....

j 'Is it a good .... for Clara to go to Dorfli?' thinks Herr Sesemann.

k 'Your daughter isn't very ....,' says Dr Classen.

GUESS WHAT

What happens in the next chapter? Match the people with the sentences.

a Heidi ...

1 stays in Frankfurt all winter.

....

b Peter ...

2 visits Heidi and her grandfather.

....

c Clara ...

3 is a very good student.

....

d Grandfather ...

4 goes for walks with the doctor every day.

....

e Dr Classen ...

5 learns to read with Heidi's help.

....

Chapter 5 ❧ Dr Classen's visit

When Herr Sesemann sees his old friend Dr Classen's sad face, suddenly he has an idea.

'Would *you* like to go to Switzerland?' he says. 'You can visit Heidi and when you return to Frankfurt, you can answer my question truly: Can my daughter Clara make this journey?'

'What a good idea!' Dr Classen says.

'Do you want to go?' asks Herr Sesemann.

'Of course,' laughs the doctor.

◖◗

summer the warmest three months of the year, between spring and autumn

Every morning that **summer** after Heidi's return, she goes up the mountain with Peter and his goats. Peter loves being with Heidi up on the mountain, but he doesn't tell her about this.

Then one morning, Heidi comes out of Grandfather's hut with an old **letter** from Clara in her hand, and she tells Peter, 'I can't go with you today. I must stay here.'

'Why?' the goatherd asks.

Heidi opens the letter and gives it to Peter. 'Because it's nearly autumn and Clara and her grandmother are coming soon. I must be here to meet them,' she says.

'But Grandfather's here. They can wait for you in the hut with *him*!' Peter says.

'No, Peter,' Heidi says. 'Clara's my best friend. I must be here when she arrives.'

Peter is angry. He says nothing, but he gives back the letter to Heidi quickly. Then he walks up the mountain after the goats.

《◎ ◎》

Not long after that, two people come up the mountain one morning. Heidi sees them from far away.

'It's Clara and her grandmother! They're here!' she cries to Grandfather. But when the people come nearer, she sees her **mistake**. They are Dr Classen and a man from the village with the doctor's bags.

letter you write this to tell something to someone

mistake when you think or do something wrong

Heidi is very sad at first about this, but she feels better when Dr Classen tells her, 'Clara and her grandmother are coming in the spring!'

The doctor likes talking to Grandfather, and they are soon good friends. They go for long walks over the beautiful mountains nearly every day. Their interesting talks, their **healthy** walks, and the mountain **air** are good for the doctor. He soon feels well again. When he returns to Frankfurt, he's a new man – a happier man.

When winter comes, Grandfather moves from his mountain hut down to his old house in Dorfli. Heidi goes to the village school. She likes learning there a lot, and she's a very good student.

The winter that year is very bad, with lots of snow. So Peter can't go down the mountain to school every day. Of course, he isn't very sad about that.

healthy something good to make ill people better and stronger

air you take this in through your mouth and nose

One day, after school, Heidi goes up the mountain to visit him and his grandmother. Their little house is very cold and dark, and Grandmother isn't feeling well. But when Heidi reads to her, the old woman smiles.

'Do you want to read to Grandmother, too?' Heidi asks Peter the next day at school. 'She'd like that, I know.'

'But how can I? I can't read. You know that,' Peter answers her angrily.

'You can learn to do it. I can teach you,' Heidi says.

And so, every afternoon, Peter visits Heidi, and she teaches him. She's a good teacher, and soon Peter can read nicely to his grandmother. This makes the old woman very happy.

⟨⊙ ⊙⟩

When the long, cold, dark winter finishes, spring comes to the mountain. Heidi feels more and more excited. Every day, she waits and watches for Clara and her grandmother. 'When are they coming?' she thinks.

READING CHECK

Choose the correct pictures.

a ... goes to Switzerland and visits Heidi.

1 ☐ Clara

2 ☐ Herr Sesemann

3 ☑ Dr Classen

b Heidi and Peter go ... every morning.

1 ☐ to school

2 ☐ up the mountains

3 ☐ to church

c ... is Dr Classen's new friend.

1 ☐ Grandfather

2 ☐ Grandmother

3 ☐ Peter

d Grandfather and Heidi stay in ... in winter.

1 ☐ the village of Dorfli

2 ☐ Frankfurt

3 ☐ the hut on the
mountain

e Heidi helps Peter when ... .

1 ☐ she reads to
Grandmother

2 ☐ she takes care of
the goats

3 ☐ she teaches him
to read

WORD WORK

1 Match the parts of the words to make words from Chapter 5.

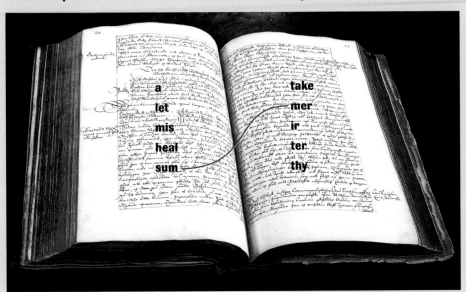

a   take
let   mer
mis   ir
heal   ter
sum   thy

2 Use the words from Activity 1 to complete the sentences.

a Heidi and Peter go out with the goats every day in ..*summer*... .

b Heidi makes a .... when she sees Dr Classen from far away.

c Clara writes a .... to Heidi about her visit.

d The mountain .... is very good for Dr Classen.

e Dr Classen feels very .... after his visit to the mountains.

GUESS WHAT

What happens in the next chapter? Tick the boxes.

		Yes	No
a	Clara and her grandmother arrive in the mountains.	☐	☐
b	Peter feels very happy when Clara visits Heidi.	☐	☐
c	One day, Peter pushes Clara's wheelchair over a cliff.	☐	☐
d	Clara feels homesick in the mountains.	☐	☐
e	Herr Sesemann takes Clara home to Frankfurt for the winter.	☐	☐
f	Heidi goes back to Frankfurt with Clara.	☐	☐

31

Chapter 6 ✤ You can walk!

In the end, the big day arrives! Heidi sees some people far down the mountain. Slowly, they come nearer. 'Clara! Grandmamma!' Heidi cries, and she runs and meets them.

'Oh, Heidi,' says Clara. 'Do you live here? It's beautiful!'

'Hello there, Heidi,' smiles Grandmamma Sesemann, and she takes Heidi in her arms.

When they reach the hut, Grandfather is waiting for them. He says 'Hello!' warmly. Soon he and Grandmamma Sesemann are talking and laughing in front of the hut. After Grandfather puts Clara in her wheelchair, Heidi takes her for a little walk. When they return, Clara can't stop talking about the beautiful mountains.

Grandmother Sesemann smiles and says, 'I'm staying in a hotel in the nearest town, but would you like to stay here in the mountains with Heidi?'

'Can I?' Clara asks.

'Yes!' says Grandfather.

'You can,' says Grandmamma.

'Oh, good!' cries Heidi excitedly.

⟪☾ ☽⟫

Clara loves her new home, and with the mountain air and healthy things to eat, she feels stronger every day. But not everybody is happy about that. Every morning, when Peter comes for Grandfather's goats, he asks Heidi, 'Are you coming up the mountain today?'

Heidi always answers, 'No. I can't **push** Clara's wheelchair up the mountain. So I must stay here with her.' That makes Peter angry.

Then one morning, Heidi smiles at Peter and says, 'Clara and I can come up the mountain with you today because Grandfather is coming too, and he can push the wheelchair!' Peter says nothing, but when nobody is looking, he takes Clara's wheelchair and he pushes it over a cliff and runs away.

push to move something quickly and strongly with your hands

'Where's my wheelchair?' cries Clara when Grandfather carries her out of the hut.

Grandfather and Heidi go and look for it everywhere, but they can't find it.

'Oh, no! Now I can't go up the mountain,' says Clara.

'Yes you can,' says Grandfather quickly, and he **carries** her up. After he puts her down carefully in a **meadow**, he goes back down and looks once more for the wheelchair. In the end he finds it down the cliff. 'Peter!' he cries.

◖◉◉◗

At first Clara is happy on the mountain, but then she sees some beautiful flowers far from her up the meadow. She feels sad because she can't walk over to them.

carry to take with you in your arms

meadow a green field with flowers in it on a hill or mountain

'I can carry you,' says Heidi.

'No, you can't. You need to be stronger for that,' Clara says to her friend.

'Wait! I've got an idea! Peter!' Heidi cries.

Slowly, Peter comes to her. 'What is it?' he says angrily.

'I want to carry Clara to the flowers. Can you help me?' Heidi asks him.

Clara stands, and Peter and Heidi take her arms. With their help, she moves slowly up the meadow. She is looking at the flowers. Suddenly, she moves away from her friends and she begins to walk alone.

'Clara,' Heidi cries, 'you can walk!'

'Oh, yes! You're right, Heidi. I can!' answers Clara.

❦

The next day, Clara's grandmother visits them. Grandfather tells her about the wheelchair. And when Clara walks in front of her, Grandmamma can't **believe** her eyes. In a hurry, she writes a quick letter to her son:

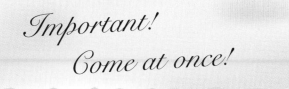

Important!
Come at once!

believe to think that something is true

Soon after that, Herr Sesemann arrives. When he is near Grandfather's hut, Clara and Heidi walk down to him. 'Clara!' he cries. 'You're walking!'

'Yes, Father, I am. You can thank Heidi and her grandfather for that!'

⟪ ⟫

Later that day, when it is nearly time for the Sesemanns to leave, Grandmamma has a quiet talk with Peter.

'You're sorry about Clara's wheelchair. I know that. And you're not a bad boy. So I'm not angry with you. Everyone can make a mistake. And now Clara doesn't need her wheelchair. She can walk! So please make a **wish**. What would you like most of all?'

'A **whistle**!' he answers.

Grandmamma laughs at that, and gives some money to him, 'With this you can buy a new whistle every week for the next fifty years, Peter,' she says.

After that, she and Herr Sesemann talk to Grandfather.

'My good friend,' Herr Sesemann says, 'How can we thank you for everything?'

'You don't need to thank me,' Grandfather says.

wish when you want something very much, and perhaps someone can give it to you

whistle something not expensive that makes a musical noise when you put air from your mouth into it

'Oh, yes, we do. Make a wish, please,' Herr Sesemann says to the old man.

'A wish? OK, but it's for Heidi, not for me.'

'For Heidi?' says Grandmamma.

'Yes. She's happier up here in the mountains than in towns or villages,' Grandfather says. 'So I want to leave my hut to her when I die.'

Herr Sesemann smiles and says, 'Then Heidi can have all the money she needs to stay here. It's our present to her. She's nearly family, after all.'

After that, Clara takes Heidi in her arms, and they say goodbye sadly.

Then Clara says, 'But I'm coming back next summer – and every summer after that, I promise.'

'See you next summer then!' laughs Heidi. 'I can't wait!'

And not long after that, Herr Sesemann, Grandmamma and Clara begin the long journey home.

READING CHECK

1 Correct the mistakes in these sentences.

    grandmother

a In the end, Clara and her ~~father~~ arrive at Grandfather's hut.

b Peter feels happy when Heidi doesn't go up the mountain with him.

c One day, Peter wants to push Clara up the mountain in her wheelchair.

d Peter pushes Clara's bag over a cliff and runs away.

e Heidi carries Clara up the mountain.

f Clara begins to read with Heidi and Peter's help.

g Heidi is sadder in the mountains than in villages or towns, Grandfather thinks.

h Clara wants to visit Heidi next year – and every year – in winter.

2 What do they say?

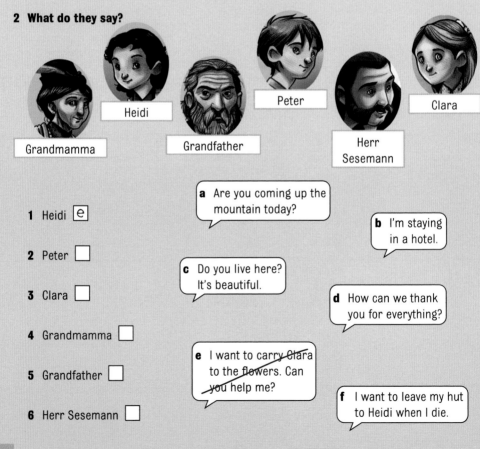

Grandmamma   Heidi   Grandfather   Peter   Herr Sesemann   Clara

1 Heidi [e]

2 Peter [ ]

3 Clara [ ]

4 Grandmamma [ ]

5 Grandfather [ ]

6 Herr Sesemann [ ]

a Are you coming up the mountain today?

b I'm staying in a hotel.

c Do you live here? It's beautiful.

d How can we thank you for everything?

e I want to carry ~~Clara~~ to the ~~flowers~~. Can ~~you~~ help me?

f I want to leave my hut to Heidi when I die.

WORD WORK

Choose the correct word in each sentence.

a Grandmamma can't (*believe*)/ *begin* it when Clara walks.

b Grandfather *carries / arrives* Clara up the mountain.

c Clara learns to walk in a *meadow / window* of flowers.

d What would you like most? Make a *finish / wish*.

e Can I *push / put* the wheelchair for you?

f Peter asks Grandmamma for a *bottle / whistle*.

GUESS WHAT

What happens after the end of the story? Finish these sentences with your own ideas.

a Heidi stays ....

....

....

b Heidi and Peter ....

....

....

c Clara goes ....

....

....

d Grandfather lives ....

....

....

Project A *Writing telegrams*

1 A telegram is a very short letter. Who sends these telegrams in the story of Heidi? Read and match.

☐ Fräulein Rottenmeier

a

ARRIVE WITH HEIDI TOMORROW.
MOTHER DEAD. CAN'T STAY WITH ME.

☐ Dr Classen

b

IN FRANKFURT. CLARA NICE.
HOUSEKEEPER BAD. MISS YOU.

☐ Dete

c

STRANGE THINGS HAPPENING HERE!
PLEASE COME HOME!

☐ Grandmamma

d

IMPORTANT! COME AT ONCE!

☐ Heidi

e

MOUNTAINS BEAUTIFUL. GOOD FOR CLARA.
SHE CAN VISIT NEXT SPRING.

2 Who gets each telegram in Activity 1?

Herr Sesemann: ☐, ☐, ☐
Grandfather: ☐, ☐

3 Write telegrams of 5–10 words for these situations.

a Herr Sesemann sends a telegram to Dete about Heidi walking in her sleep.

b Heidi sends a telegram to Grandfather about coming home.

c Brigitte sends a telegram to her sister with news of Heidi's return.

d Herr Sesemann sends a telegram to Fräulein Rottenmeier about Clara walking.

4 Play a telegram writing game.

- Think of some news.
- Write a telegram with the news. Sign your name.
- Give your telegram to your teacher.
- Your teacher gives out the telegrams.
- Read your classmate's telegram. Write a reply.

Project B *Magnificent mountains*

1 Match definitions a–h with the numbered words.

8 range

1 summit

2 peak

a ☐ this takes people quickly up mountains

b ☐ a slow river of ice

c ☐ this person climbs mountains

d ☐ the pointed top of a mountain

e ☐ a number of mountains together

f ☐ a long, thin edge of a mountain

g ☐ a wall of rock

h ☐ the highest part of a mountain

5 rock face

3 ridge

4 cable car

7 glacier

6 mountaineer

2 Read about the Matterhorn on page 43. Complete the notes below.

Height: ....

Mountain range: ....

Location: ....

Nearest villages: ....

Number of climbers every year: ....

Easiest route: .... Time: ....

Hardest route: .... Time: ....

THE MATTERHORN

The Matterhorn is a mountain in the Pennine Alps between Switzerland and Italy. It's 4,478 metres high and is one of the highest peaks in the Alps. The nearest villages are Zermatt in Switzerland and Cervinia in Italy.

The Matterhorn is famous all over the world. You can see it on posters, chocolate bars, and souvenir boxes. The peak has four steep rock faces – the north, east, south and west faces. All around it there are glaciers. More than 3,000 mountaineers reach the summit every year, but it isn't easy. The easiest way to go up it is the Hörnli route up the north-east ridge. It takes about six hours to climb from the Hörnli hut. The hardest route is the south face. It takes about 15 hours and is very difficult.

Zermatt is a very special village. There are no cars there, but there are mountain trains, a cog railway, and lots of cable cars. This stops pollution. It's a great place for skiing and other winter sports, even in the summer.

The Hörnli route

3 Complete the text about Mount Fuji with the information in the table. Use a dictionary to help you.

Height:	highest in Japan – 3,776 metres
Mountain range:	not part of one – it's a volcano
Location:	west of Tokyo on Honshu Island, Japan
Nearest city:	Tokyo
Japanese names:	'Fujiyama' or 'Fuji-san'
Number of climbers:	over 200,000 people every year
Routes up mountain:	4 – divided into 10 stations
Easiest route:	Drive or take bus to 5th station, then walk to summit.
Time:	about 5 hours

Mount Fuji is ...the highest mountain in Japan....
It's .... high. Mount Fuji isn't part of
...., it's a
.... It's on .... You can see
the mountain from the city on a good day. It's called
.... in Japanese.
There is snow on the peak for many months of the year.

There are many famous pictures of Mount Fuji and there are lots of poems about it, too.
There are four .... the mountain. The walk is divided ....
stations. Most people .... or .... halfway up the mountain to
.... station and then .... This takes .... hours.
More than .... every year!

4 Choose another famous mountain and find out more about it. Use the table in Activity 3 to help you make notes. Then write about your mountain.

Ararat   Popocatépetl   Sinai

Everest   OLYMPUS   Kilimanjaro

GRAMMAR CHECK

To + infinitive or –*ing* form of verb

After the verbs *finish*, *go*, *like*, *love*, *miss* and *stop*, we use verb + –ing.

Heidi loves reading.

After the verbs *forget*, *learn*, *need*, *promise*, *remember*, *want* and *would like*, we use to + infinitive.

I'd like to read that book.

With the verbs *begin* and *like*, we can use verb + –ing or to + infinitive.

1 Complete the sentences about the story with the to + infinitive or verb + –ing form of the verbs in brackets.

a Dete stops ....taking.... (take) care of Heidi when she finds new work.

b She finishes .... (visit) Grandfather very quickly.

c She forgets .... (say) 'thank you' to him.

d Grandfather doesn't like .... (talk) much.

e He loves .... (make) things with his hands.

f Heidi needs .... (have) a new little chair because there isn't one in the hut.

g She wants .... (sleep) up in the hayloft.

h Peter goes .... (walk) in the mountains every day.

i Heidi would like .... (go) up the mountain with Peter and the goats.

j Peter begins .... (hit) one of the goats.

k Heidi promises .... (give) some of her lunch to Peter every day.

l That night, she remembers .... (take) her lunch with her.

m She doesn't miss .... (live) with Aunt Dete.

GRAMMAR CHECK

Need and don't/doesn't need

We use need + to + infinitive without *to* to talk about something that is necessary.

'You need to fix Grandmother's old house,' Heidi tells her grandfather.

Grandfather needs to work on the house for some days.

We use don't/doesn't need + to + infinitive to talk about something that is not necessary.

'You don't need to ask me again, Heidi,' says Grandfather.

Heidi doesn't need to help her grandfather with the work.

2 **Complete each sentence with the correct form of *need* and one of the verbs in the box.**

(not) cry	(not) go	help	lie	leave
sleep	(not) speak	~~take~~	take	tell

a Peter .needs .to .take . care of the goats when they're up the mountain.

b 'I always .... down when I'm tired,' says Peter.

c 'I .... to school in summer,' smiles Peter.

d Peter .... the mountain in winter because he goes to school.

e Grandfather .... Heidi to visit Peter's grandmother because the old woman lives down near the village.

f Grandfather .... to Brigitte and her mother so he leaves Heidi at the door of their house.

g 'I .... my mother a lot because she's very old,' says Brigitte.

h Brigitte .... her mother about Heidi because she can't see the girl.

i 'You ...., Heidi,' says Peter's grandmother. 'I'm OK.'

j Peter's grandmother .... at night, but the noisy old house stops her.

Possessive adjectives

We use possessive adjectives to show that somebody or something belongs to somebody when we do not use the owner's name.

Herr Sesemann is Clara's father. = *Herr Sesemann is her father.*

Heidi is Grandfather's granddaughter. = *Heidi is his granddaughter.*

The Sesemanns' house is wonderful. = *Their house is wonderful.*

3 **Write possessive adjectives for the underlined words.**

her	his	~~his~~	its	my	our	their	your

a <u>the pastor's</u> visit ..... his ..... visit

b <u>the goat's</u> feet .... feet

c <u>the villagers'</u> houses .... houses

d '<u>Heidi's</u> hand,' Aunt Dete tells Heidi. .... hand

e '<u>The Sesemanns'</u> friends,' say the Sesemanns. .... friends

f <u>Herr Sesemann's</u> work .... work

g <u>Clara's</u> wheelchair .... wheelchair

h '<u>Clara's</u> late mother,' says Clara. .... late mother

4 **Complete the sentences with the correct possessive adjectives.**

a 'I can't send .... my ..... granddaughter down the mountain in winter!' says Grandfather to the pastor.

b The pastor looks at Grandfather with a smile on .... face.

c 'But you can live in .... old house in Dorfli,' he answers the old man.

d '............. granddaughter can't read or write,' Dete tells Grandfather.

e Herr Sesemann has lots of money, but .... daughter is very ill.

f Heidi doesn't want to go with .... aunt.

g The Sesemanns live with .... housekeeper, Fräulein Rottenmeier.

h 'It's wonderful to have Heidi in .... house!' Clara tells Fräulein Rottenmeier.

i 'I miss .... home in the mountains,' thinks Heidi.

j Clara loves .... little white kitten with .... nice green eyes.

k Heidi doesn't like Fräulein Rottenmeier or .... angry eyes.

GRAMMAR CHECK

Prepositions of movement

Prepositions of movement tell us how something moves.

up ↗	down ↘	into ■→
out of ■→	across ◢↗	past →•
through ⇒	to →•	from •→

5 **Complete the text with the prepositions in the box.**

across   down   from   from   from   through
into   out of   ~~out of~~   past   to   up

Heidi looks **a)** ....out of.... her window, but she
can't see any mountains **b)** .... there.
Some days later, she finds the Sesemanns' front
door open, and she walks **c)** .... the
house alone. She runs **d)** .... the streets
of Frankfurt and **e)** .... many different
buildings. She's looking for a tall tower. In the
end, she finds a church tower, and a nice man
takes her **f)** .... it. He takes care of
the church and he has a room there. Heidi looks
g) .... the town, but she can't see any
mountains at all **h)** .... the tower –
only lots of houses in front of her! After that,
Heidi comes **i)** .... the tower, and the
man goes **j)** .... his room for a minute.
Heidi takes two kittens **k)** .... him,
and she hurries back **l)** .... the
Sesemanns' house.

GRAMMAR CHECK

Adverbs of manner

We use adverbs of manner to talk about how we do things.

Heidi is leaving the house quietly.   *'Answer me,' says Fräulein Rottenmeier angrily.*

To make regular adverbs, we add –ly to the adjective.	**Adjectives that end in –y, change to –ily.**
quiet – quietly	*angry – angrily*

Some adverbs are irregular.

He understands Heidi well. (adjective = good)   *She speaks very fast. (adjective = fast)*

6 Complete these sentences with adverbs of manner.

a Fräulein Rottenmeier looks ....𝖽𝖺𝗋𝗄𝗅𝗒.... (dark) at Heidi.

b The little girl walks .... (slow) back to her room.

c Heidi misses her grandfather .... (bad).

d 'My father's back home,' cries Clara .... (excited).

e Herr Sesemann talks to Heidi .... (nice).

f He stops Fräulein Rottenmeier .... (quick).

g Heidi learns to read .... (happy) with Grandmamma's help.

h The girls say goodbye to Grandmamma very .... (sad).

i .... (strange), the front door is open every morning.

j The servants can't see the ghost in the hall very .... (good).

k Herr Sesemann hurries home .... (fast) when he hears about the ghost.

l .... (sudden), Herr Sesemann and Dr Classen hear a noise.

m The doctor listens .... (careful) to Heidi.

GRAMMAR

GRAMMAR CHECK

Comparative adjectives

We add –er to make the comparative form of most short adjectives.

tall – taller

When adjectives end in –e, we add –r.

nice – nicer

When adjectives end in a short vowel + consonant, we double the last consonant and add –er.

big – bigger

When adjectives end in consonant + –y, we change y to i and add –er.

happy – happier

With longer adjectives (other 2 syllable adjectives, or adjectives with 3 syllables or more), we put more before the adjective to make the comparative form.

interesting   more interesting

Some adjectives have an irregular comparative form.

good – better   bad – worse   far – further

7 **Complete the sentences with the adjectives in brackets in the comparative form.**

a Heidi is ..healthier.. (healthy) than Clara.

b Heidi is a .... (good) student than Peter.

c Heidi is .... (happy) in Dorfli than in Frankfurt.

d Heidi is .... (nice) to Clara than Peter.

e Peter is .... (big) than the girls.

f Peter is .... (interested) in Heidi than in Clara.

g Peter is .... (angry) than before when Clara arrives in Dorfli one spring day.

h Clara is .... (sad) than before when Heidi leaves Frankfurt for Switzerland.

i Clara is .... (hungry) in Dorfli than in Frankfurt.

j Clara is .... (tall) than Heidi.

k Clara is .... (interesting) for Heidi than Peter.

l Things are .... (bad) for Peter than for Heidi.

m Grandfather's hut is .... (far) up the mountain than Grandmother's house.

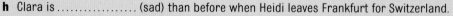

n Grandfather is .... (strong) than all three of the children.